PERFECT PETS

Big Dogs

Linda Jacobs Altman

BENCHMARK BOOKS

MARSHALL CAVENDISH

NEW YORK

Benchmark Books
Marshall Cavendish Corporation
99 White Plains Road
Tarrytown, New York 10591

Library of Congress Cataloging-in-Publication Data
Altman, Linda Jacobs, date.
Big Dogs / Linda Jacobs Altman.
p. cm. — (Perfect Pets)
Includes bibliographical references (p.   ).
Summary: Provides information about the history, physical
characteristics, choice, training and care of various breeds of
large dogs.
ISBN 0-7614-1101-1 (lib. bdg.)
1. Dogs—Juvenile literature. [1.Dogs. 2.Pets.] I. Title. II. Series.
SF426.5 .A49   2001   636.7 dc21   99-049674   CIP   AC

Photo research by Candlepants, Inc.

Cover photo: *Animals Animals:* Robert Pearcy
Back cover photo: *Photo Researchers, Inc.:* Renee Lynn

The photographs in this book are used by permission and
through the courtesy of: *Animals Animals:* Lynn M. Stone,
title page; Don Enger, 3; Norvia Behling, 4; Donna Ikenberry,
8; Michael Habicht, 9; Gerard Lacz, 10, 12, 13 (bottom), 13 (top);
Robert Maier, 14, 15; FritzPrenzel, 16; Zig Leszczynski, 18; Ulrike
Schanz, 19; Renee Stockdale, 20; Richard Kolar, 26 (bottom);
O.S.F., 26 (top); Joe McDonald, 27; Bill Silliker, Jr., 28; *Art
Resource:* Erich Lessing, 7; *Corbis/Bettmann:* 6; *Michele Noone:*
24 (bottom), 24 (top); *Photo Researchers, Inc.:* Andrew
J. Martinez, 22; Renee Lynn, 30; *Photofest:* 25.

Printed in Hong Kong
6   5   4   3   2   1

*For Jasmine, who is big,
and for Oscar, who thinks he is.*

Mixed-breed dogs, like these three friends, make wonderful pets.

Big Dogs

have been helping humans for thousands of years. They work as guide dogs, guard dogs, hunting dogs, and herding dogs. They help policemen track down criminals. They help search-and-rescue teams find lost hikers.

St. Bernards are famous for rescue work. These gentle giants come from the mountains of Switzerland, where the snow is deep and the winters are long. In the mid-1800s, one of these St. Bernards became a legend.

His name was Barry. He risked his life many times to rescue people who got lost in the snow. Barry would use his huge paws to clear away snow from a victim. Then he would lie close to keep the person warm. His deep bark called human helpers. At least forty people owed their lives to this brave dog.

In this painting, the famous dogs of Hospice of St. Bernard rescue a snowbound traveler. One dog barks to call for human help, while the other tries to waken the victim.

The people of the mountains have never forgotten Barry. Whenever a new litter of St. Bernards is born, one puppy is chosen to carry his name. There has been a Barry in the Swiss mountains for 150 years. There always will be.

Newfoundlands take to the water the way St. Bernards take to the snow. Newfoundlands are famous for rescuing drowning swimmers. In the 1800s, every lifeguard station in England kept a pair of Newfoundlands. They were an important part of the stations' lifesaving equipment.

When a swimmer got into trouble, the dogs went to work. They would swim out to the victim and let him or her grab

Odysseus and His Dog

The Greek poet Homer wrote about a hero's long journey home from war. The voyage of Odysseus lasted almost twenty years. When he finally returned, he had changed so much that nobody recognized him.

Nobody, that is, but his dog Argos. At the sound of his master's voice, the old hound raised his head and wagged his tail. For a moment, dog and man looked at one another. Then Argos laid down his head and died.

The dog Argos is a symbol of loyalty. He alone recognized Odysseus when the hero returned home after twenty years. This famous statue captures the moment.

hold. If the victim couldn't hang on, each dog would grab an arm. They always kept the person's face out of the water as they headed back to shore.

Most big dogs like taking care of someone. This can lead to some unusual friendships. A German shepherd named Bear surprised his owners by "adopting" an African pygmy goat. The owners expected trouble when they brought the

Big dogs often carry packs. The pack on this Samoyed might be filled with first-aid supplies, food, or tools.

Pit bulls are often used as guard dogs. This is not because they are naturally mean. It is because they are strong and learn quickly.

baby goat home. They thought Bear might try to hurt it.

Instead, Bear and the goat, whose name was Stormy, became best friends. Bear protected Stormy from other animals. The two played together, ate together, and slept together.

Their favorite game was leapfrog. They would chase around the yard, raising a ruckus and jumping over each other's backs. Their antics always got a laugh.

German shepherds are natural protectors. They help humans in many ways: as police dogs, guide dogs for the blind, guard dogs, and family pets.

Dogs

can be **purebred** or **mixed breed**. Purebreds have parents and ancestors of only one **breed**. Mixed dogs have parents and ancestors of two or more breeds.

The American Kennel Club (AKC) keeps records on purebred dogs. It recognizes 148 breeds in seven groups: sporting, hound, working, terrier, toy, nonsporting, and herding. There is also a miscellaneous class for breeds that have not yet been included in one of the main groups. Most big breeds belong to the sporting, hound, working, or herding groups.

Sporting dogs are sometimes called hunting dogs, bird dogs, or retrievers. The sporting group includes breeds such as the Labrador retriever, golden retriever, and Irish setter. These dogs were bred to help hunters find and flush out **game**. They also make great family pets. They are loyal, eager to please, and always willing to play.

Hounds are trackers. Some rely on sight and speed to

The bull mastiff is a combination of two older breeds: the giant mastiff and the bulldog. The result is a powerful dog with a fierce appearance.

The Biggest Dog in the World

In 1989, a mastiff named Zorba made the *Guinness Book of World Records* as the world's largest dog. At 343 pounds (154 kilograms), Zorba outweighed most football linemen. From his nose to the tip of his tail, he was more than eight feet long (about two and a half meters). If Zorba stretched out on a king-size bed, his nose would hang over one end and his tail over the other.

chase down their prey. Others use their noses. The sad-faced bloodhound is the best-known of the scent hounds.

Bloodhounds usually work in packs. One sniff of a piece of clothing or other personal article, and they are off. They fan out, sniffing the ground for a telltale scent. When they find it, they race ahead. Heads up and long ears flapping, they bay into the wind. Baying is a sound halfway between a bark and a howl. It lets their human partners know that the game is near.

Above: *Retrievers are popular hunting dogs. They also make good playmates for children.*

Left: *Boxers belong to the working group of dogs. They are born with flopped ears. The ears are cropped to make them stand up. This gives the dog a more fearsome appearance.*

Sight hounds are tall dogs with long legs and slim bodies. The sleek greyhound is the best-known member of this group. Greyhounds are the fastest dogs in the world. They can average more than thirty miles (forty-eight kilometers) per hour over distances up to one mile (about one and a half kilometers). That is above the speed limit for cars passing through a school zone.

With its long legs and sleek body, the greyhound is born to run. Greyhounds are the favored breed of dog racing enthusiasts.

Dogs in the working group help their humans in many ways. They act as guards, rescuers, companions, and protectors. The working group includes many of the giant breeds, such as the St. Bernard, mastiff (MASS-tif), Great Dane, and New-foundland. These magnificent dogs outweigh many full-grown men. They can rest their chin on the dinner table without even stretching.

Herding dogs were originally bred to care for sheep—and sometimes cattle—in the fields. They are protective and clever. A good sheepdog can move a flock from paddock to pasture and back again. It can rescue stragglers and drive away wolves or other predators.

Why Your Dog Raises Its Hackles

The hair along the neck and spine of a dog bristles, or stands up, when the dog scents prey or confronts an enemy. This happens because the hair shafts are connected to tiny muscles. When these muscles tighten, they raise the hairs.

When a dog raises its hackles, its whole body tenses. The ears go forward. The tail stops wagging. When a guard dog confronts someone in this way it is a warning: *Don't* come a step closer or you will be attacked.

German shepherds were originally bred as herding dogs. This shepherd circles the flock to stop any sheep from straying.

The sheer size of Great Danes makes people respect "Beware of Dog" signs.

Dogs

share a common ancestry with jackals, foxes, coyotes, and wolves. All are members of the **canine** family. Like their wild cousins, dogs have keen senses. They see in dim light much better than humans can. They hear sounds that are too high-pitched for human ears. Some breeds can catch a scent from one-quarter mile (almost one-half kilometer) away. That's the distance of almost four and a half football fields placed end to end.

The long friendship between dogs and humans started about ten thousand years ago. People began adopting and taming wolf cubs. They soon learned that these animals could be more than pets. They could be loyal friends and companions. They could help with many kinds of work.

Over time, these tamed wolves evolved into dogs. Soon, different breeds appeared. Each breed became suited to the

Sled dogs like this Siberian husky are strong enough to pull heavy loads over snow and ice. A thick coat helps protect them from the cold.

work it was to do. For example, breeds that worked in water developed sleek, waterproof coats. Sight hounds developed keen eyes and long legs so they could see over a wide area.

All dogs learn to communicate with humans. They can understand spoken commands and follow instructions. They can "tell" their humans what they want and need.

Opposite: *The spotted dalmatian is the traditional "firehouse dog." Newborn puppies are solid white, with perhaps a patch of color on the ears. The spots appear later.*

Dogs do this in many ways. They wag their tails when they are happy and bare their teeth when they are angry. They make different sounds for different situations. A "Hi, how are you?" bark does not sound the same as a warning bark. A growl can be playful.

Behaviors also say a great deal. When a dog wants to go outside, it might stand at the door and bark. When it wants to be petted, it might lay its head in someone's lap.

The life span of a dog is much shorter than that of a human being. A dog is an adult by the time it is one year old. The normal life span for small breeds is about fifteen years. For large breeds, it is about ten years. Giant breeds, such as the Great Dane and St. Bernard, often do not live beyond their eighth year.

Opposite: *Puppies are naturally adventurous. This yellow Labrador retriever pup has found a forbidden "treasure."*

In quiet moments, a puppy may give a preview of the dignified adult it will become.

Bringing

a new puppy into the household is always an adventure. To get your puppy off to a good start, set rules early and stick to them. If you don't want the puppy to go into certain rooms, put up portable gates or close the doors. If the sofa or your dad's favorite chair is going to be off-limits, don't let the puppy sit there.

You don't have to scold. Just say "no" in a firm but gentle voice. Then pick up the puppy and set it on the floor. If you do this every time, your new friend will get the idea.

Careful training is especially important for big breeds. Behaviors that are only annoying in little dogs can be dangerous in big ones. For example, a little dog that jumps up on people may snag a stocking or leave dirt on a pants leg. A big dog can knock somebody down a flight of stairs.

Sleeping and chewing are favorite activities of growing puppies. Teething puppies will chew on anything, from bedroom slippers to telephones.

Besides training, all dogs need regular care. Some dog-care chores must be done every day. These include feeding the dog, keeping its water bowl full, and cleaning its toilet area. Long-haired breeds need a daily brushing, and all breeds need daily exercise.

Young puppies should have about four meals a day. They

Superstar Dog: Rin-Tin-Tin

During World War I, Lee Duncan was an American soldier serving in France. In 1918, Duncan found a German shepherd puppy in a bombed-out building. He named the puppy Rin-Tin-Tin. When the war ended, Duncan brought "Rinty" home with him.

That was the beginning of a legend. Rin-Tin-Tin became a movie star. Rinty and his descendants made twenty-two movies. Rin-Tin-Tin IV had his own television show during the 1950s.

Today, Rinty has a fan club on the Internet. A breeder in Texas has carried on the line. People come from all over the world to buy a puppy that is a descendant of Rin-Tin-Tin.

Millions of these "autographed" pictures of Rin-Tin-Tin have gone out to fans all over the world.

can't eat enough at one meal to keep up with their fast-growing bodies. Adult dogs should be fed twice a day. This is especially important with some of the largest breeds. They can develop serious stomach problems from eating too much at a single meal.

Dogs should always have plenty of fresh water on hand.

A sturdy doghouse gives shelter from bad weather and a comfortable place to sleep all year long.

Grooming is an important part of dog care. Here, a black Labrador gets groomed while its feline friend looks on.

27

Retrievers love to fetch anything from the daily paper to a stick at the beach.

Also be sure your dog has all its shots. One of the first things to do with a new puppy is take it to the **veterinarian**. He or she will examine the puppy to be sure it's healthy and will give it a series of puppy shots. Adult dogs need yearly boosters to keep them protected against certain diseases.

Finally, there is one other thing a dog needs—plenty of love and attention. Play with your dog. Rub its tummy. Scratch behind its ears. Let it sit with you while you do homework or watch TV. Let it walk with you when you go outside.

All these things take time, but it is time well spent. If you take care of your dog, you will not only have a good pet, but you will also have a loyal and loving friend.

Playing with Your Big Dog

Big dogs love to play, especially when they're young. You have to be careful what games you teach them, though. Wrestling is out because you could get hurt. Tug-of-war is also out, unless you don't mind losing all the time.

Big dogs are bred to work, and they like to feel useful. Teach your dog to do a special job. Some of the giant breeds can pull a little cart. This is handy for gardening, doing errands, or taking a picnic basket to the lake.

The sporting breeds love to fetch. Throw a stick, a ball, or a Frisbee, and the dog will chase it down. With a little training, your dog will even fetch foul balls at Little League practice.

Fun Facts

- There are 54 million pet dogs in North America.

- North Americans spend $10 billion a year on medical care for their pets.

- Puppies develop inside their mothers for sixty-two to sixty-three days. Average litter size is three to six puppies. Dogs are fully adult at the age of one year.

- Dogs are blind to the colors red and green.

- The eye of a dog has three lids: an upper, a lower, and an inner lid. The inner lid sweeps across the eye from the inside corner, acting like a windshield wiper.

- Dogs have forty-two teeth.

- The length of a muzzle (nose) varies greatly from breed to breed. For example, the German shepherd's muzzle is about eight inches (twenty centimeters) long. The bull mastiff's is only one to three inches (three to seven centimeters) long.

Glossary

breed: A group of animals that are descended from the same ancestors and share the same basic characteristics, including the way they look.

canine: Of or belonging to the dog family of animals.

game: Wild animals that are hunted for food or sport.

mixed breed: A dog whose parents and ancestors are not of the same breed.

purebred: A dog whose parents and ancestors are of the same breed.

veterinarian: A doctor who takes care of animals.

Find Out More About Big Dogs

American Kennel Club. *The Complete Dog Book for Kids*. New York: Howell Book House, 1996.

Benjamin, Carol Lee. *Dog Training for Kids*. New York: Howell Book House, 1988.

Evans, Mark. *ASPCA Pet Care Guide for Kids: Puppy*. New York: Dorling Kindersley, 1993.

Rin-Tin-Tin Fan Club: http://www.rintintin.org/fanclub.htm

Index

About the Author

Linda Jacobs Altman lives in the small town of Clearlake, California. She and her husband, Richard, share their home with four dogs, four cats, and two cockatiels. Ms. Altman has written many books for young people, including *Small Dogs*, a title in the Benchmark *Perfect Pets* series.

CHRISTOPHER CHURCHMOUSE CLASSICS™

A SUNDAY SURPRISE

"You will know how people ought to conduct themselves in God's household" — 1 Timothy 3:15 (NIV).

WRITTEN BY BARBARA DAVOLL

Pictures by Dennis Hockerman

A Sonflower Book

VICTOR BOOKS®

A DIVISION OF SCRIPTURE PRESS PUBLICATIONS INC.
USA CANADA ENGLAND

To W. B. B. C. Library,
Barbara Davoll

Christopher

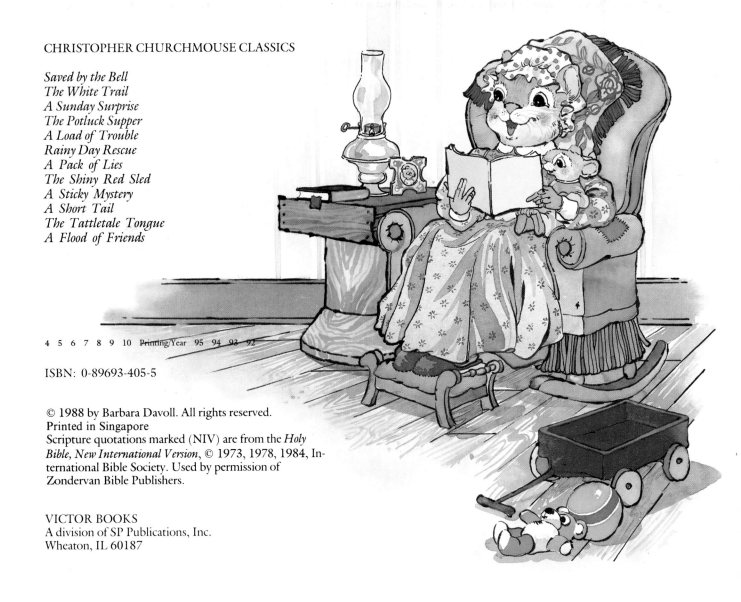

CHRISTOPHER CHURCHMOUSE CLASSICS

Saved by the Bell
The White Trail
A Sunday Surprise
The Potluck Supper
A Load of Trouble
Rainy Day Rescue
A Pack of Lies
The Shiny Red Sled
A Sticky Mystery
A Short Tail
The Tattletale Tongue
A Flood of Friends

4 5 6 7 8 9 10 Printing/Year 95 94 93 92

ISBN: 0-89693-405-5

VICTOR BOOKS
A division of SP Publications, Inc.
Wheaton, IL 60187

A Word to Parents and Teachers

Children will grow in their knowledge of the Lord as they enjoy the delightful Christopher Churchmouse series.

This book, *A Sunday Surprise,* one of the character-building stories in the series, is about good behavior.

"I am writing you these instructions so that . . . you will know how people ought to conduct themselves in God's household"
—1 Timothy 3:15 (NIV).

Christopher's observation of misbehavior and Ned's sad experience will show children how one's actions affect others.

The Discussion Starters will help children make practical application of the biblical truth.

Christopher's Friend,

Barbara Davoll

Christopher Churchmouse sat in his favorite Sunday morning place, hidden in the soft heavy folds of the red velvet window curtain. He looked over the church filled with people. From his hiding place he could see everything and what he saw amazed him.

It's the first day of spring weather, thought Christopher. *Maybe that's why the children are behaving so very badly in church.*

Billy Stern, sitting between his mother and his sister Suzie, was acting the worst of all. He was running a very noisy toy truck along the back of the pew in front of him. Christopher could see it was annoying the people sitting in front of Billy, for they kept turning around and glaring at him.

Click, clack, click, clack, click, clack, went the toy. Billy paid no attention at all to those who were staring at him.

Why doesn't Mrs. Stern do something about the noise her son is making? Christopher wondered. *Maybe she is hard of hearing. Surely she has taught Billy to behave in church! Why, it's awful, the disturbance he's causing!*

Just ahead of the Sterns sat two little girls who were talking, giggling, and acting very silly.

Can't someone tell them to be quiet? Christopher kept hoping, but no one did. *These children are behaving much worse than my mice friends ever would!*

From across the aisle came a crackling noise that sounded like fire. Christopher was ready to jump and run when he saw it wasn't a fire at all. Some children were eating candy and rattling their candy bags.

Do they know how much noise they are making? Christopher wondered, as he watched them put one candy after another into their mouths. *Why, even the mice children were not allowed to touch any crumbs they might find when the church service was in progress.*

Christopher was disgusted!

"These children are very naughty!" he said to himself. "I can't believe the way they behave in church!"

Just then there was a loud POP on the other side of Billy Stern. Christopher was so surprised he nearly fell out of his hiding place in the curtain. What he saw was a strange sight. A boy sitting near Billy had his cheeks puffed out. The boy stuck out his tongue with some gum on it, and then blew.

As Christopher watched in

amazement, a great round ball came out of the boy's mouth. It grew bigger and bigger—then POP! The ball had burst and the boy was picking the gum off his face and eyes and poking it back into his mouth again.

"What is that?" exclaimed Christo-pher. He had never seen bubble gum before. "Why doesn't he just chew the stuff up and swallow it? Sometimes people are really hard to understand. We mice could teach them a thing or two about behaving in church."

Then the organ began to play. This was one of Christopher's favorite times in church, for he loved the beautiful music. Some men were passing offering plates down each row. Christopher knew the people were putting money into the offering plates because they loved the Lord and wanted to give to His work.

Leaning way out, Christopher saw the men passing the offering plate to the people sitting in front of the Stern family. Soon the plate would be passed to Mrs. Stern.

Squinting his eyes to see better, Christopher saw something long and brown in the plate of money. "That looks like a mouse tail," he said to himself.

Peering closely, he saw to his horror that the tail belonged to his smallest cousin, Ned, who was sound asleep in the offering plate. Ned's tiny tail was sticking out over the plate and his plump little body was covered with money. Apparently, the people hadn't even noticed him as they passed the plate and dropped in their money. He was very tiny and still and about the same color as the velvet lining of the plate.

Christopher knew naughty Ned must have been playing in the plates and had fallen asleep. Chris was frantic! What could he do? Ned would surely be discovered soon. What an awful predicament!

Now the man was passing the plate to Mrs. Stern. Just as she took the plate, Ned moved and stretched his little legs.

Christopher had no time to think. As Mrs. Stern saw the little mouse, she screamed and jumped up quickly, upsetting the plate of money and knocking down the man who had passed it to her. The money clanged and jangled as it rolled underneath the pews.

Christopher stretched too far out of the curtain and fell to the floor. There was so much commotion he hardly knew what to do. Billy and Suzie Stern had set up a yowl. Mrs. Stern was shrieking and hopping around in the aisle. Several ladies had climbed up on to the seats, holding up their skirts and screaming.

Shaking himself off from the fall, Christopher shouted to Ned, who by this time was awake. "Let's get out of here!" squeaked Christopher.

Christopher grabbed Ned's paw and together they ran as fast as their legs could go. Down the aisle and out into the hall ran the two little mice. They could still hear the women screaming, and the pastor trying to bring order back to the service. The way home seemed endless as they raced along.

13

Darting into Christopher's little hole-in-the-wall home, they slumped to the floor to catch their breaths. Just then the door opened. They were startled to see the whole Churchmouse family staring in at them from the hall.

Mama and Papa Churchmouse were standing quietly in the doorway.

Ned's papa and mama, Uncle Rootie and Aunt Snootie, were there, too, with all of their mice children trailing behind them. All the mice had very solemn faces, even Grandma and Grandpa Churchmouse. Christopher's little friend Mandy Mouse was there, looking very sad and disappointed.

14

Papa Churchmouse was the first to speak. "What happened up there?" he asked in a serious voice.

Christopher did not want to tell on Ned, but he didn't see how he could help it.

"Well, sir," he squeaked unhappily, "you—you see, Ned fell asleep in the money plate, and Mrs. Stern saw him and screamed. Then everything happened! She jumped up. The man got knocked down, and . . ."

"And the whole church service was disturbed," said Papa. "Oh, I'm so ashamed! I thought we had taught you mice to behave better than that!"

"But, Papa," said Christopher, "it wasn't my fault. I was just sitting there when it all happened. Besides, we were much better than the children. They were

talking, eating candy, blowing bubble gum, and even playing with toys in church. They were awful!"

"Don't compare yourselves to them," said Papa. "They must answer for their bad behavior. You mice caused much more of a disturbance than the children. You interrupted the whole church service."

Christopher and Ned hung their heads in shame.

"I'm sure Ned didn't mean to fall asleep in the offering plate," said Christopher helpfully.

"No, but our misbehavior always catches up with us," said Uncle Rootie. "Ned knows better than to play in the church sanctuary. That is where the people worship God. I'm afraid there is one little mouse who hasn't learned how to behave himself yet," Uncle Rootie said, taking Ned firmly by the paw. "I think that lesson had better be learned right now." With that, he took Ned to their own little home for the correction he needed.

The rest of the family disappeared to their own homes too, except for Grandpa and Grandma, who stood looking thoughtfully at Christopher.

Hanging his head, Christopher said, "I'm so ashamed. I really didn't

mean any harm, but now everyone will think I did. I don't ever want to go back again."

Grandpa laid his hand kindly on Christopher's shoulder. "I wouldn't feel like that if I were you," he said.

"You wouldn't?" questioned Christopher.

"No, my boy," said Grandpa.

"There's a lesson to be learned from all of this. For some of us the lessons come harder than others. You'll feel better about it soon. Just see that *you* do what is right, *yourself*, and don't worry about what others do and think."

"Yes, Grandpa," replied Christopher meekly.

Grandpa and Grandma went to their own home then, leaving Christopher with his mother and father. Christopher was feeling very sad.

Then Papa said, "I know you're feeling badly about this morning."

"Oh, yes, Papa," replied Christopher. "I just feel awful! Everyone will remember what happened, and they'll know I'm Ned's cousin," said Christopher unhappily.

Papa said, "Come sit with me, Chris, while Mama fixes our lunch."

Papa sat down in his big chair,

and although Christopher was growing up, he climbed onto Papa's lap.

Then Christopher's kind papa explained to him that people should not go to church to be seen by others. He told Christopher that the church building is a place to worship and

hear about God. Papa said that people came to church to learn about God, "And that's very important for boys and girls and men and women. We must be very quiet and respectful in church. Then we won't disturb anyone and keep them from hearing the truth from God's Word."

As Papa talked, Christopher began to understand why it was so necessary to be quiet and not disturb the service.

When Mama called them to lunch, Christopher was snuggled up fast asleep on Papa's lap.

"Well, Papa," she asked, "did you have a good talk?"

"Yes," said Papa, smiling, "and I think he'll be a much wiser mouse. Now he really understands why it is so important to behave properly in church."

22

DISCUSSION STARTERS

1. Where was Christopher when he heard the noisy children?
2. What did the boy have on his tongue or in his mouth?
3. Why was Ned in the plate of money?
4. Why did Christopher not want to go back into the church sanctuary?
5. See if you can remember what Papa Churchmouse said about behaving in church.
6. What were some of the children doing? Do you ever do any of those things?

   Did this story help you think about how you should act in church?